Sou...

Italy

Text from: *Pasta. All the Recipes* (2012), *The Cuisine of Italy. All the Recipes* (1999), edited by Giunti Editore.

Translation: Helen Clearly and Helen Galve for Lexis, Florence; Lexis, Florence.

Layout & Graphic Design: Cinzia Chiari
Editorial Staff: Alessandra Pelagotti

www.giunti.it

© 2014 Giunti Editore S.p.A.
Via Bolognese 165 - 50139 Florence - Italy
Piazza Virgilio 4 - 20123 Milan - Italy
First edition: January 2014

Reprint	Year
6 5 4 3 2 1	2019 2018 2017 2016 2015

Printed by Giunti Industrie Grafiche S.p.A. - Prato (Italy)

passion
for
PASTA

GIUNTI DEMETRA

CONTENTS

CONTENTS

PASTA, VEGETABLES AND CHEESE

FRESH PASTA AND GNOCCHI

CONTENTS

INTRODUCTION

ITALY = PASTA

The invention of pasta, a dough made of cereal mixed with water, goes back a long way. Traces of this food have been found in Etruscan bas-reliefs, and in Greek and Roman texts. What is certain is that dry pasta was eaten during the Arab domination of Southern Italy, long before Marco Polo came back from the Orient (1292) with his tales of Chinese soya spaghetti.

Pasta has become a symbol of Italy the world over, and the red-white-and-green dish of spaghetti is recognised everywhere as a message of joy and good cooking.

THE RIGHT SAUCE

A plate of pasta does not make up a large part of our daily calorie allowance (100 g dry pasta = 200-250 g cooked pasta = 360 calories). But this does not permit us to eat as much as we want. Smaller helpings of pasta, from 60 to 80 grams, can be followed by moderate portions of other foods, giving our body everything it needs without overdoing it.

9

Sauces and added ingredients should be chosen carefully, Substituting a sauce or reducing its amount is mainly a question of taste.

The recipes found on the following pages appear in their traditional versions. For instance, you will find lard as well as butter. Whenever possible, use **extra-virgin olive oil** as a substitute, and always cold-pressed. This type of oil provides a dressing that is rich in unsaturated fatty acids. Due to its chemical composition, it undergoes only minor alterations in cooking, which are harmless.

PASTA: TYPES AND FORMATS

Pasta is simply the result of mixing water with flour (obtained by milling wheat). There are two types of wheat: **durum wheat**, which when milled produces *semola* and *semolato*, and common wheat, which when milled gives white flour. Since durum wheat is more expensive, it is usually mixed with **common wheat**. Italian law specifies that the dry pasta sold in shops cannot have more than 7% common wheat flour, while foreign brands entirely ignore this restriction.

Good quality dry pasta is recognisable by its yellowish colour, its slightly sweet flavour and the fact that it is odourless. It can be stored for a long time in a dry, dark place. Fresh pasta can be kept for a shorter time (a few days only) and should be refrigerated. The packets should be kept closed to protect against dust and insects.

Whole-grain pasta deserves special mention. This factory-made pasta is left untreated by refining processes. Refinement deprives the flour of those natural properties of the wheat that make it a balanced element: protein, sugar, fats and mineral salts, vitamins and enzymes. Be careful, however, to choose only whole-grain pasta produced from wheat grown without the use of toxic products, which leave a residue on the grains of wheat.

Further care should be taken to choose pasta that is really made of whole-grain flour and not merely common flour to which bran has been added. The latter will not have a uniform amber colour but rather a freckled appearance that reveals the presence of added bran.

Both regular and whole-grain pasta are found in the shops. Their different characteristics appear on the labels.

• **Regular, dry pasta:** produced with durum wheat flour.

• **Dry egg pasta:** this includes 200 g of eggs for each kilo of flour.

• **Coloured fresh or dry pasta:** made of flour coloured with a percentage of spinach, powdered tomatoes, tomato concentrate or eggs (200 g per kilogram of flour).

• **Special dry pasta:** produced with flour to which has been added a percentage of malt or gluten to increase the protein value to 15-20%.

• **Fresh pasta:** can be made of durum wheat flour alone, common wheat flour alone, a combination of both, and/or other ingredients.

In Italy, it seems, there are 500 different pasta formats, and still today imaginative producers are creating more new types. In general, the formats available can be grouped as follows:

• **Long, rounded pasta** with varying diameters (*vermicelli*, *spaghettini*), and sometimes hollow (*bucatini*, *zite*);

• **Long narrow ribbon-like pasta** such as *trenette*, *linguine*, *bavette*;

• **Long, wide pasta:** *lasagne*, *pappardelle*, *reginette*;

• **'Nests' or 'coils' of pasta:** *capelli d'angelo*, *fettuccine*, *tagliolini*, *tagliatelle*;

• **Medium-short pasta:** *penne*, *conchiglie*, *ruote*;

• **Short, thick pasta:** *maccheroni*, *sedanini*, *fusilli*.

RULES FOR A GOOD PLATE OF PASTA

• Choose the pasta format in relation to the sauce you plan to make: the bigger the pasta, the richer the sauce.

• The pasta should be cooked in plenty of water (around 1 litre for each 100 g). If you are cooking less than half a kilo of pasta, the pasta/water ratio changes; for example for 4 people calculate 350 g pasta and 4 litres of water. Bring the water to the boil in a large, deep pot so that the heat is evenly distributed. The liquid should never reach the brim of the pot because pasta can swell to three times its dry volume while cooking.

• Add salt only when the water has begun to boil, calculating about 10 g salt for every litre of water. Salted water, in fact, boils at a lower temperature than fresh water.

• Add the pasta to the pot when the water is already boiling. As soon as the water comes to a boil again, lower the heat to a simmer. An exception to this rule is filled pasta, which is added to the pot a minute before boiling so that it will not be broken by the motion of the water.

• Stir the pasta regularly so that it cooks evenly and does not stick. A useful hint, especially for egg or filled pasta, is to pour a little oil in the water before adding the pasta.

• Drain the pasta when it is *al dente*; the less water it absorbs, the tastier and more digestible it will be. If the pasta is to be tossed in the pan or baked au gratin in the oven, drain it slightly before it is fully cooked.

For the cooking time, apart from the indications given on the packet, you can trust in the old 'taste test' (if there is a little white dot in the middle of the spaghetti, it needs to be cooked 1 minute longer).

• Having turned off the heat, stop the cooking process by pouring a glass of cold water into the pot, then drain the pasta in a colander. If you are cooking gnocchi or another delicate pasta, drain with the aid of a slotted spoon or a large fork, transfer to a deep dish, tip up and let the excess water drain out with the help of a lid.

If the pasta is to be tossed in the sauce, or if stipulated in the recipe, leave it in a little of its cooking water so that it will mix better with the sauce.

• Traditionally, pasta is dressed in the following sequence: drain the pasta, transfer it to a serving bowl with some grated cheese in it (optional), then fold in the sauce, mixing gently and carefully to blend the ingredients.

CARE WITH OTHER INGREDIENTS

Some final words of advice before you begin to cook. All the ingredients, not just the main ones, should be **fresh** and of the **best quality**. Make sure that fish, in particular, is fresh, and caught in clean water.

Nature offers the cook an inexhaustible source of flavours in the form of **aromatic herbs**. Garlic, basil, bay leaves, fennel, mint, marjoram, hot red peppers, etc., are small but very important ingredients. Do not mix too many aromatic herbs together in the same dish, and always use them in moderation, so as not to overwhelm the flavour of the other ingredients.

The salt used in the following recipes is **sea-salt**, now readily available in both the coarse and the fine form. This salt, not subjected to refinement processes, is rich in elements such as chlorine, sodium, magnesium, sulphur, calcium, potassium, bromine, carbon, strontium, silicon, fluoride, zinc, phosphorous, etc.

14

CONVERSION CHART

WEIGHT AND LENGHT	CORRESPONDES TO
1 gram (g)	0.035 ounces (oz) divide by 28 to find ounces
1 hectogram (hg)	3.57 ounces (oz) divide by 0.28 to find ounces
1 kilogram (kg)	2.2 pounds (lb) divide by 0.45 to find pounds
1 millilitre (ml)	0.03 fluid ounces (fl oz) divide by 30 to find fluid ounces
1 litre (l)	2.1 pints (pt) multiple by 2.1 to find pints 3.8 gallons (U.S.) (gal) divide by 0.26 to find U.S. gallons 0.22 gallons (U.K.)(gal) divide by 4.5 to find U.K. gallons
1 centimeter (cm)	0.4 inches (in) multiple by 0.4 to find inches
1 millimeter (mm)	0.04 inches(in) multiple by 0.04 to find inches
1 meter (m)	3.3 feet (ft) multiple by 3.3 to find feet
TEMPERATURE	
Celsius degree (°C)	180 °C = 356 °F (°C x 1.8) + 32 to find Farenheit degree
Farenheit degree (°F)	392 °F = 200 °C (°C -32) x 555 to find Celsius degree

NOTE

The quantities in the recipes
on the following pages are for 4-6 servings.

God MADE
FOOD,
the devil
THE **COOKS.**

James Joyce

PASTA WITH MEAT

Amatriciana
Bucatini

400 g bucatini,
200 g bacon,
300 g ripe and firm
tomatoes, 1/2 onion,
extra-virgin olive
oil, grated pecorino,
salt, ground hot red
pepper

Blanch the tomatoes in hot water, peel them, remove the seeds and chop.

Chop the bacon and brown it in several table-spoons of oil. As soon as the fat has rendered, remove the bacon from the pan and set aside.

Chop and sauté the onion in the same oil. Add the tomatoes and salt, and let the sauce thicken for about ten minutes. Put the cooked bacon back in the sauce and flavour with ground hot red pepper.

Use the sauce to flavour the bucatini, cooked in boiling salted water and drained when al dente. Sprinkle generously with grated pecorino.

Since the original recipe had little or no tomato, this ingredient can be omitted if preferred.

400 g tagliatelle
(recipe on page 122),
200 g ground beef,
50 g bacon,
1/2 onion, 1 small
carrot, 1/2 celery
stick, 1 1/2 tablespoons
tomato concentrate,
1/2 glass red wine,
grated Parmesan
cheese, stock,
extra-virgin olive oil,
salt and pepper

Tagliatelle with Bolognese Sauce

Finely slice the onion, carrot and celery. Slice the bacon and brown it in a few teaspoons of oil (not too much oil if the bacon is fatty). When the fat has rendered, add the chopped vegetables, stirring gently.

As soon as the vegetables have wilted, add the meat. Keep stirring until the meat is evenly browned. Add the wine and let it evaporate.

Add the tomato concentrate, diluted with a little hot stock and seasoned with salt and pepper. Lower the heat and simmer covered for about 2 hours. Moisten from time to time with a little hot stock.

Boil the tagliatelle, drain when al dente, and mix with some of the meat sauce. Serve with the remaining sauce in a sauce boat, and grated Parmesan on the side.

There are several variations to this dish. You can use mixed ground meats, or add some chopped chicken liver with dry mushrooms and the water used for steeping, or omit the tomato concentrate, and so on.

Fettuccine alla Papalina

Sauté the chopped onion in a few tablespoons of oil over high heat, add the peas and season with salt and pepper.

Lower the heat, cover and let simmer, adding a little hot water from time to time if necessary. Just before removing the pan from the heat, cut the ham into smaller slices and add to the peas.

In the meantime, beat the eggs together with the Parmesan, a pinch of salt and some freshly ground pepper in a warmed serving bowl.

Cook the pasta, drain when al dente, pour into the warmed bowl and add the pea sauce. Mix well before serving.

400 g fettuccine (recipe on page 122), 100 g thinly sliced Parma ham, 200 g small peas, 2 eggs, 1/2 onion, 2 1/2 tablespoons grated Parmesan, extra-virgin olive oil, salt, freshly ground pepper

Farfalle with Turkey Sauce

400 g farfalle (butterfly-shaped pasta), 200 g turkey breast, 100 g bacon, 500 g ripe and firm tomatoes, 200 g fresh hulled peas, 1 onion, marjoram, extra-virgin olive oil, salt and pepper

Chop the onion and sauté it with the chopped bacon in several teaspoons of oil.

Cut the turkey into thin slices and add it, stirring gently to let the flavours blend.

Soften the peas in boiling salted water, then add them in.

Blanch the tomatoes in boiling water, peel them, remove the seeds, chop and cook together with the peas. Let the sauce thicken; season it with salt, pepper and marjoram.

Continue cooking, adding a few drops of water from time to time if the sauce becomes too dry.

Cook the farfalle in boiling salted water, drain when al dente and mix with the sauce.

Garganelli alla Boscaiola

400 g garganelli (recipe on page 120), 200 g porcini mushrooms, 150 g thick-cut bacon, 4 ripe tomatoes, 1 clove garlic, 30 g butter, 1 sprig parsley, Parmesan cheese, salt and pepper

Clean the mushrooms with a soft brush or a damp rag without rinsing in water. Sauté the sliced mushrooms, chopped bacon and crushed garlic in butter over medium heat, while stirring with a wooden spoon.

Blanch the tomatoes in hot water, peel them, remove the seeds, chop and add them to the mushrooms and bacon. Cook over low heat until the sauce has thickened and remove the garlic.

Boil the garganelli in abundant salted water, drain when al dente and transfer to a large serving dish.

Add the sauce, garnish with chopped parsley and sprinkle generously with grated Parmesan. Serve immediately.

Maccheroni with Sausage

Skin the sausage and brown it over low heat in its own fat. Cream the ricotta in a large bowl with salt, a generous grinding of pepper and the sausage.

When the mixture is rich and creamy, set it aside and cook the pasta in abundant salted water.

Drain the maccheroni when al dente, reserving a few spoonfuls of the cooking water.

Transfer the pasta to a serving dish with the ricotta and sausage mixture and mix carefully with the salted water, a sprinkling of grated pecorino and a drizzle of oil.

400 g maccheroni,
400 g ricotta cheese,
150 g sausage, grated
pecorino cheese,
extra-virgin olive oil,
salt and pepper

Fusilli with Sausage and Mushrooms

400 g fusilli (short, curly pasta),
200 g sausage,
300 g fresh porcini mushrooms
or 30 g dried porcini mushrooms,
300 g tomato pulp, 1 onion, 1 small carrot, 1 bay leaf,
marjoram,
extra-virgin olive oil,
salt and pepper

Clean the mushrooms carefully and dice. If you are using dried mushrooms, steep them first in lukewarm water. Chop the onion and carrot and sauté them in a few tablespoons of oil. When the onion is transparent, add the skinned and sliced sausage, the mushrooms and the crushed bay leaf.

Cook for a few minutes stirring gently, then add the tomato pulp, salt and pepper. Lower the heat, cover the pot and simmer until the sauce has thickened. If necessary, add some hot water or stock from time to time (or use the liquid in which the mushrooms have been steeping, strained through a cotton cloth). Before removing from the heat, flavour the sauce with finely chopped marjoram.

For a different flavour, combine the sausage with artichokes. Remove the spiny ends and tough outer leaves from the artichokes, cut into wedges and soak in water and lemon juice before adding to the mixture of onion and carrot in the pot. In either case, the sauce used to dress the fusilli should be very hot.

PASTA
WITH MEAT

Pappardelle with Hare Sauce

400 g pappardelle
(recipe on page 122),
1 small hare,
50 g bacon,
1/2 onion,
1/2 celery stick,
1 small carrot, 1 clove
garlic, rosemary,
2 teaspoons tomato
concentrate
(or 1.5 dl milk),
1 glass red wine,
extra-virgin olive oil,
salt and pepper

Clean the hare, keeping the forepart (head and shoulders), heart and liver for the sauce. Wash under cold running water, dry and cut into pieces, being careful not to break the bones.

In a few tablespoons of oil, sauté a mixture of chopped bacon, garlic, onion, carrots and celery. As soon as the vegetables begin to wilt, add the pieces of hare, including the entrails.

Allow meat to brown over moderate heat, add the wine and let it evaporate. Season with salt, pepper and rosemary.

Continue cooking for a few minutes, then add the tomato concentrate diluted in a little hot water. Lower the heat, cover the pot and simmer for about half an hour. If necessary, add a little stock or hot water from time to time.

When the meat is done, take the pieces of hare out of the pot, remove the bones, and chop. Pass the sauce through a sieve, then put back over the heat, with the chopped meat and entrails. Heat the sauce well before mixing in the pasta, which has been cooked in boiling salted water and drained when al dente.

Pici with Rabbit Sauce

400 g pici (recipe
on page 119),
1/2 rabbit,
300 g tomato sauce,
100 g bacon,
2 celery sticks,
1 onion, 1 carrot,
2 cloves garlic, 2 bay
leaves, 1/2 litre red
wine, extra-virgin
olive oil, salt and
pepper

In a large dish, marinate the rabbit overnight in the wine with the aromatic herbs and the coarsely chopped vegetables. Next day, remove the vegetables, chop them finely and sauté in a little oil with some chopped bacon. Remove the rabbit from the marinade, cut it into pieces and add to the sautéed mixture.

Stir to let the rabbit meat absorb the flavours, then moisten with wine from the marinade and let it evaporate almost entirely.

Add the tomato sauce, season to taste, cover the pot and simmer over moderate heat for about an hour and a half. When the sauce is done, remove the rabbit, bone it and cut the meat into smaller pieces.

Blend the cooking juices to a creamy sauce, then put the pieces of meat back in it. Set aside to rest while you prepare the pasta. Boil the pici in salted water and drain when al dente. Put the sauce back over the heat, add the pasta and toss together for one minute.

29

Pappardelle with Wild Boar

400 g pappardelle (recipe on page 122), 400 g coarsely ground lean wild boar meat, 350 g tomato pulp, 2 teaspoons tomato concentrate, 1 small carrot, 1 onion, 1 celery stick, 2 bay leaves, 1 glass of red wine, extra-virgin olive oil, salt, ground hot red pepper

In a little oil, sauté a mixture of finely chopped onion, carrot and celery, add the ground meat and let brown.

Add the red wine and let it evaporate. Mix in the tomato pulp and the tomato concentrate diluted in a little hot water.

Add salt, ground hot red pepper and the bay leaves. Simmer over low heat for about an hour and a half.

Boil the pappardelle in salted water, drain when al dente and stir in the meat sauce before serving.

A variation to this recipe suggests using 2 parts boar meat and 1 part beef to lessen the gamy flavour typical of wild boar. You can also use only tomato concentrate, omitting the tomato pulp.

Reginette with Speck

400 g reginette,
200 g thickly sliced
speck (cured smoked
ham), 100 g fresh
hulled peas,
2 cloves garlic,
1/2 glass dry white
wine, extra-virgin
olive oil, grated
Parmesan cheese,
salt and pepper

Blanch the peas in boiling salted water for about ten minutes, then drain. Cut the speck into cubes and sauté in a few tablespoons of oil with the sliced garlic cloves and the peas. As soon as the garlic begins to colour, remove it from the pan.

Add the wine to the peas and let it evaporate. Add salt and pepper and continue cooking over moderate heat for about ten minutes.

In the meantime, cook the reginette in abundant salted water, drain when al dente and transfer to the pot with the speck and peas.

Mix together over the heat for a few minutes, season with a grinding of pepper and sprinkle with grated cheese.

To vary this recipe, add 3-4 tablespoons of cream to the speck to bind the mixture together.

Spaghetti alla Chitarra al Ragù

Chop two cloves of garlic with a little parsley, then mix with the chopped bacon fat and a little freshly ground pepper to form a paste. Spread the paste over the slice of pork, beaten thin with a meat pounder or the blade of a knife.

Place the bacon slices over the paste and top with a few pieces of pecorino. Roll up the meat and fasten with toothpicks or kitchen thread.

Cut the remaining lard into pieces and melt in an earthenware pot along with the remaining garlic clove. Brown the meat, add a little wine and as soon as it has evaporated add salt and pepper.

Peel the tomatoes, discard the seeds, chop and add to the meat. Cook the sauce until done. A minute before turning off the heat, remove the meat and set it aside.

Boil the spaghetti in salted water, drain when al dente and flavour with the sauce. Slice the meat and serve it as a second course.

400 g spaghetti
alla chitarra,
500 g pork in 1 slice,
4 slices of bacon,
1 piece of bacon fat,
500 g ripe
and firm tomatoes,
3 garlic cloves,
a small bunch parsley,
red wine,
1 tablespoon lard,
fresh pecorino, salt
and pepper

Bucatini with Lamb and Peppers

400 g bucatini,
200 g lamb,
500 g tomato pulp,
2 red or yellow
peppers, 2 cloves
garlic, 1 bay leaf,
1/2 glass dry white
wine, extra-virgin
olive oil, salt, ground
hot red pepper

In an earthenware pot, protected by a heat diffusing plate, flavour several tablespoons of oil with crushed garlic and a bay leaf, then add the diced lamb and let it brown. Remove the garlic cloves and add the wine, letting it evaporate over high heat.

Clean the peppers, remove seeds and inner filaments, finely chop, and add to the lamb. Cook for a few minutes, then add the tomato pulp. Bring the sauce to the boil over high heat, then lower the heat, cover and simmer until the meat is done.

Before removing from the heat, check the seasoning and flavour with ground hot red pepper.

Cook the bucatini in abundant salted water, drain when al dente, and drizzle with oil. Transfer to a serving dish and dress with the sauce.

400 g spaghetti,
200 g bacon,
2 eggs and 2 egg
yolks, 1 clove garlic,
2 tablespoons
grated Parmesan
cheese, 1 tablespoon
grated pecorino,
extra-virgin olive oil,
salt and pepper

Spaghetti Carbonara

Dice the bacon into 5 mm cubes and brown in a pan with a few tablespoons of oil and the clove of garlic (removing the garlic as soon as it begins to colour).

In a warmed serving bowl, beat 2 whole eggs and 2 yolks at room temperature with the grated cheeses. Season with a pinch of salt and plenty of freshly ground pepper, and stir well to form a smooth, creamy sauce.

The sauce should be prepared when the pasta is almost done. Boil and drain the pasta, transfer it to the serving bowl, mix with the egg and the crunchy hot bacon and serve piping hot.

There IS NO
LOVE
more **sincere**
THAN THE *LOVE*
of **FOOD.**

George Bernard Shaw

PASTA
WITH FISH

Bavette
with Fish

400 g bavette, 600 g mixed seafood such as baby squid, small cuttlefish, scampi and shrimp, 3 cloves garlic, a small bunch parsley, 1/2 glass of white wine, extra-virgin olive oil, salt, ground hot red pepper

Remove any small bones or fins from the seafood as well as eyes, beaks or entrails (extracted by pulling the tentacles, taking care not to break the ink sac, which can be used to flavour this or another sauce).

Wash the seafood and if the bodies are large, cut them into small strips, leaving the little tentacles intact. Shellfish need not be shelled, just washed carefully. Cut the shrimp into pieces; the flesh can be eaten and the shell gives flavour.

In a large pot, heat a few tablespoons of oil with the crushed garlic and the hot red pepper; add the fish, heat it on all sides, then add the wine and let it evaporate.

In the traditional recipe, the bavette are broken, added to the pan with the fish along with some boiling water, and cooked like risotto.

If this seems too complicated, boil the pasta as usual, drain when al dente and mix into the sauce before serving. In either cases, stir in a generous sprinkling of chopped parsley just before turning off the heat.

400 g tagliolini
(recipe on page 122),
3 slices of bottarga,
1/2 clove garlic,
1 small bunch parsley,
the juice of 1/2
lemon, extra-virgin
olive oil, pepper

Tagliolini with Bottarga

Bottarga is salted mullet roe and looks like a kind of hard greyish-brown salami. It can be sliced thin and used to prepare canapés, or grated like Parmesan over a plate of pasta.

The following recipe suggests another way to use bottarga as a garnish for pasta. Boil the pasta in abundant salted water. In the meantime, sauté the bottarga in 2 tablespoons of oil and a little of the pasta water.

As soon as the bottarga has melted, add the lemon juice. Drain the tagliolini when al dente and mix into the bottarga, sprinkle with pepper, and a mixture of chopped parsley and garlic.

Bigoli with Sardines

400 g bigoli
(recipe on page 120),
6 sardines,
1 clove garlic,
a small bunch parsley,
1 glass of extra-
virgin olive oil, salt

In this typical dish from the Veneto Region, the sardines used in the traditional recipe were always fished in Lake Garda.

You can, however, use tinned sardines, which should be cleaned (without using water, if possible), deboned, and then treated like fresh ones.

Clean the sardines, removing the heads, bones and tails; wash them, let them dry on a teacloth, then cut them into small pieces.

Cook them in hot oil until they begin to disintegrate. Just before turning off the heat, add a mixture of chopped garlic and parsley.

Boil the bigoli in salted water, drain while still al dente and blend thoroughly into the sauce.

Fettuccine with Crab

400 g fettuccine
(recipe on page 122),
4 crabs,
1 small onion,
1 clove garlic,
40 g wild fennel,
200 g ripe
tomatoes, dry white
wine, extra-virgin
olive oil, salt

The original recipe calls for 'gnacchere', molluscs found off the Sardinian coast with a beautiful shell. However, gnacchere taste almost exactly like crab meat, which is more readily available. Crab meat can thus be used without changing the taste of this recipe in any way.

Blanch the tomatoes in hot water for a few seconds, remove the skins and seeds and cut into cubes. Finely chop the onion and garlic.

Scoop out the crab meat and cut it into pieces. Sauté the onion and garlic in the oil, add the wine and let it evaporate, then add the crab.

Cook for a few minutes over moderate heat, remove from the heat and add the tomatoes. In a pot with a little lightly salted water, boil the fennel for 10 minutes, add the pasta and cook together. The liquid should be almost entirely dried up.

Drain the pasta, mix into the sauce, salt to taste and add the oil. Mix carefully and serve.

Penne
with Salmon

400 g penne,
200 g sliced
smoked salmon,
50 g peeled
pistachios,
10 walnuts,
1 small onion,
1 egg yolk, cognac,
extra-virgin olive oil,
salt, freshly-ground
pepper

Chop the onion finely, chop the walnuts and pistachios more coarsely, then sauté all together in a large saucepan with a few spoonfuls of oil.

After a few minutes, pour in a little cognac and let it evaporate, then add the salmon cut into small strips, along with a twist of freshly-ground pepper. Let the flavours blend for a few moments, then remove from the heat.

In a large serving bowl, mix the egg yolk with a few spoonfuls of oil and a pinch of salt. Pour the pasta (boiled, and drained while still al dente) into the bowl, pour the salmon sauce over it, and mix all the ingredients thoroughly before serving.

In a variation of this recipe, a quarter litre of fresh table cream is used instead of the egg yolk.

46

Orecchiette with Sardines

Clean the sardines, remove the bones and cut into slices.

Prepare a mixture of chopped leek, garlic, hot red pepper, a little parsley and the anchovy fillet and sauté it in oil. Add the sardines and cook until golden brown. Add the pine nuts, tomato sauce and saffron. Continue to cook over low heat.

Cook the pasta, drain and transfer to the pot with the sauce. Sauté for a few minutes.

Remove from the heat, garnish with the chopped parsley and serve immediately.

400 g orecchiette (recipe on page 119),
200 g sardines,
20 g pine nuts,
1 ladle of tomato sauce, 1 anchovy fillet in oil,
1 clove garlic, 1 leek,
1 small bunch parsley,
1/4 teaspoon saffron,
1/2 hot red pepper,
extra-virgin olive oil,
pepper

47

Pasta Sicilian-Style

400 g maccheroncini,
350 g fresh sardines,
200 g wild fennel,
80 g anchovies in oil,
30 g pine nuts,
30 g raisins,
2 cloves of garlic,
3 1/2 tablespoons extra-virgin olive oil,
2 teaspoons chopped parsley, 2 teaspoons breadcrumbs,
saffron, ground hot red pepper, salt and pepper

Clean the sardines, wash and leave to dry on a tea-cloth. Cook the fennel for a few minutes in a little salted water; drain and dice. Soak the raisins in lukewarm water for 15 minutes.

Crush the garlic and sauté in a few tablespoons of oil over low heat. As soon as the garlic begins to colour, remove and add the sardines. Brown on both sides. Add the fennel, the drained raisins, pine nuts, chopped parsley, breadcrumbs, salt and hot red pepper. Continue cooking, gently shaking the pot so as to shift the sauce without breaking the fish; when the sardines are done, remove from the pot and set aside.

Add the anchovies to the pan with a pinch of saffron diluted in a little water. Cook for a few minutes until the anchovies melt.

Boil the maccheroncini in salted water (preferably the water used to cook the fennel). Drain when al dente. Place layers of pasta in an oven dish, alternating with the sauce and the sardines. Finish with a layer of pasta and a layer of sauce. Bake in the oven at 392 °F (200 °C) for about 20 minutes. Serve piping hot.

Trofie
with Squid

400 g trofie
(400 g extra-fine
flour, water, salt)
400 g squid,
1 cup of tomato
sauce, 1 sprig basil,
1 small onion,
1 clove garlic, 1 glass
dry white wine,
1/2 hot red pepper,
extra-virgin olive
oil, salt

Pour the flour onto the breadboard, add a pinch of salt and enough water to mix. Knead throughly with your hands until you have a dense, smooth, elastic dough.

Break off pieces about the size of a bean, roll them into thin sausages, then, with well-floured hands, twist them into corkscrew shapes. Leave them to dry on a flour-sprinkled teacloth for 4 hours before cooking.

Skin and remove the bone from the squid, wash in running water, and remove the tentacles. Cut the body into strips.

Sauté a mixture of sliced onion, garlic and crushed hot red pepper in oil. Add the strips of squid and the tentacles, which have been diced and salted. Add the white wine; when it has evaporated, add the tomato sauce. Simmer over low heat.

Cook the pasta in abundant salted water, drain, and transfer to the pan with the sauce. Toss for a couple of minutes, then remove from the heat.

Sprinkle with the chopped fresh basil and serve.

Tagliatelle with Trout

Sauté the finely chopped onion in a little olive oil, add the trout fillets cut into strips, and cover with white wine. Let the wine evaporate, then add the tomatoes cut into pieces and the zucchini sliced in thin disks.

Season with salt and pepper and continue to simmer over low heat.

In the meantime, boil the tagliatelle in abundant salted water, drain when al dente and serve mixed with the trout.

400 g tagliatelle
(recipe on page 122),
250 g trout fillets,
4 peeled tomatoes,
3 zucchini,
1 small onion,
dry white wine,
extra-virgin olive oil,
salt and pepper

Spaghetti with Clams

400 g spaghetti, 1 kg clams, 2 cloves garlic, a small bunch parsley, dry white wine (optional), extra-virgin olive oil, salt, 1 hot red pepper

Clean the shellfish under cold running water, then soak in salted water for half an hour to get rid of any sand. This is very important and should be done with care, as the sauce will not be strained.

In a large pan, heat several tablespoons of oil, 1 chopped garlic clove, the hot red pepper and a little wine if desired. Add the clams, cover the pan and let the clams open.

In the meantime cook the spaghetti in salted water, drain when al dente and transfer to the pan with the clams.

Mix over low heat and sprinkle with a mixture of chopped garlic and parsley. Remove from the heat and serve.

Spaghetti with Red Clams Sauce

400 g spaghetti,
500 g clams,
500 g tomato pulp,
2 cloves garlic,
a small bunch parsley,
1/2 glass of extra-
virgin olive oil, salt,
1 small hot red
pepper

Wash the clams carefully and leave for half an hour in salted water to remove any sand.

In a large pan, heat the oil with the garlic cloves and as soon as they begin to colour, remove them and add the tomato pulp.

Cook a few minutes over high heat, then lower the heat, add salt and the hot red pepper. When the sauce has thickened, add the clams.

Boil the spaghetti in plenty of salted water, drain when al dente and mix with the clam sauce and a sprinkle of chopped parsley.

Stir over the heat for a few minutes to let the flavours blend.

Tagliolini with Caviar

Place the caviar in a bowl and add a few drops of lemon juice.

Soften the butter at room temperature, chop into small pieces and mix in a large serving bowl with the cream, which has been slightly warmed.

Boil the tagliolini and drain when al dente.

Transfer to the serving dish and mix carefully with the butter and cream; stir in the caviar and some freshly ground pepper.

400 g tagliolini
(recipe on page 122),
1 small jar caviar or
lumpfish roe,
the juice of 1 lemon,
15 dl single cream,
80 g butter, freshly
ground pepper

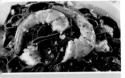

Black Tagliatelle with King Prawns

400 g black tagliatelle (basic recipe on page 122), 8 king prawns, 1 clove garlic, 1 small bunch parsley, 1 glass dry white wine, extra-virgin olive oil, salt

Prepare the pasta dough and colour it using only 3 eggs and adding the strained contents of 2 cuttlefish ink sacs diluited in a little white wine. Sauté the shelled prawns in oil, flavouring with chopped parsley, garlic and a pinch of salt. Add the white wine and cook over high heat for three minutes.

Boil the pasta in abundant salted water, drain when al dente and transfer to the pan with the sauce.

Mix carefully for a few minutes and remove from the heat. Serve piping hot and garnish with the remaining finely chopped parsley.

God MADE
only WATER,
but man
MADE WINE.

Victor Hugo

PASTA,
VEGETABLES
AND CHEESE

400 g spaghetti,
800 g ripe and firm
tomatoes,
a few basil leaves,
1 teaspoon sugar,
extra-virgin olive oil,
salt, ground hot red
pepper

Spaghetti with Tomato Sauce

This is probably the most classic of traditional sauces with a tomato base: 'pommarola', considered the sauce par excellence for accompanying pasta. Wash the tomatoes, blanch them in boiling water, peel them, remove the seeds and stalks, and pass them through a food mill. If there is too much water, leave the tomatoes on a sloping surface for about 15 minutes to let the excess liquid drain off, then cook over moderate heat with a little oil.

Simmer until the mixture thickens (about 30 minutes), seasoning with a pinch of salt and a teaspoon of sugar (to reduce the acid taste of the tomatoes).

Just before turning off the heat, add the hot red pepper and crushed basil. Boil the spaghetti and drain when al dente. Then serve in individual portions, each with a generous amount of sauce and a drizzle of olive oil.

Bucatini Funghi e Pinoli

400 g bucatini,
500 g fresh
mushrooms,
300 g tomato pulp,
1 clove garlic, 1 small
bunch parsley,
2 teaspoons
pine nuts,
1/2 glass of dry
white wine, extra-
virgin olive oil, salt
and pepper

How you clean the mushrooms will depend on the kind you use. Remove the soil from the heads and stems with a damp cloth. If the mushrooms are large, slice them and sauté the slices in a pot with oil and chopped garlic. Let them brown, add the wine, and as soon as it has evaporated, add the tomato pulp and season with salt and pepper. Lower the heat and simmer, covered for about 15 minutes.

In the meantime, brown the pine nuts and the chopped parsley in a little oil. Add them to the mushrooms, stirring gently to let the flavours blend.

Mix in the pasta, which has been cooked until al dente and then drained.

Bigoli
alla Puttanesca

Rinse the capers in running water, pit the olives, and clean the salt and bones from the anchovies. Heat some oil in a pan, add the tomatoes, capers, olives and anchovies.

Cook over high heat for 10-15 minutes, stirring frequently. Just before removing from the heat, check the seasoning, add a little hot red pepper and sprinkle with finely chopped parsley.

Boil the bigoli in abundant salted water, drain when al dente, and mix well with the sauce before serving.

400 g bigoli (recipe on page 120),
500 g tomato pulp,
1 1/2 tablespoons salted capers,
100 g black olives,
2 cloves garlic,
1 small bunch parsley,
2 salted anchovies,
extra-virgin olive oil,
salt, ground hot red pepper

Linguine
with Cauliflower

400 g linguine,
1 onion,
1 medium-sized
cauliflower,
80 g raisins,
80 g pine nuts,
salt, pepper,
extra-virgin olive oil,
grated Parmesan
cheese (optional)

Soak the raisins in lukewarm water. In the meantime, clean the cauliflower, boil in a little salted water, drain while still very firm and cut into small pieces. In a pan, sauté the chopped onion in a little oil for a few minutes, then add the cauliflower and pine nuts.

Drain the raisins and squeeze out the moisture. Add them, together with a little of the water they have soaked in, to the cauliflower and onion. Add a pinch of salt and one of pepper, and simmer over moderate heat.

Boil the pasta in plenty of salted water and when al dente, drain and transfer to a large serving bowl with half of the sauce. Bring to the table and drizzle the individual portions with the remaining sauce.

Serve grated Parmesan on the side.

400 g farfalle,
40 g red and yellow
peppers, 400 g ripe
and firm tomatoes,
2 cloves garlic,
50 g salted capers,
a few leaves of basil,
extra-virgin olive oil,
salt, ground hot red
pepper

Farfalle with Peppers

Clean the peppers, removing the seeds and filaments. Place them on an oiled tray in a hot oven to wilt, then remove the scorched outer film. Cut the peppers into strips, reserving any cooking liquid.

Heat a few tablespoons of oil with the crushed garlic; as soon as it begins to brown, remove it and add the peppers with their sauce. Cook for a few minutes, then add the tomatoes (first peel them, remove the seeds and chop coarsely).

After about 10 minutes over high heat, add the capers, which have been rinsed under running water and then dried. Add salt, and a minute or two before turning off the heat, a pinch of hot red pepper and some crushed basil leaves.

Boil the farfalle in plenty of salted water, drain, and serve with the sauce.

Fusilli with Four Cheeses

In a small non-stick saucepan, melt the Gorgonzola, Fontina, Taleggio and Gruyère cut into small cubes together with a little milk. Stir constantly over low heat.

Dilute the sauce with cream and flavour with salt, Parmesan and freshly ground pepper. Stir constantly to form a fluid, creamy sauce.

In the meantime, cook the pasta, drain when al dente and mix into the melted cheese.

Serve with grated Parmesan.

400 g fusilli (curly pasta),
100 g sweet Gorgonzola,
100 g Fontina,
100 g Gruyère,
100 g Taleggio,
milk, 1/2 glass cream,
grated Parmesan cheese, salt and pepper

Pasta with Lentils

400 g whole-grain pasta (any short pasta will do),
200 g whole lentils,
1 carrot, 1 celery stick,
2 cloves garlic,
2 bay leaves,
1 bunch parsley,
ground hot red pepper,
extra-virgin olive oil, salt

Soak the lentils for 12 hours. Drain, rinse, and cook in plenty of salted water along with the diced celery, diced carrot and bay leaves.

Cover the pot and simmer over moderate heat. When the lentils are almost done, add the pasta. Remove from the heat when the pasta is al dente.

Transfer to a large serving bowl and dress with a sauce made of oil, chopped parsley, finely chopped garlic, and ground hot red pepper, all cooked for 15 minutes over moderate heat.

400 g orecchiette
(recipe on page 119),
300 g broccoli,
2 cloves garlic,
2 teaspoons raisins
(optional), 2 salted
anchovies,
grated pecorino,
extra-virgin olive oil,
salt, ground hot red
pepper

Orecchiette with Broccoli

Wash the broccoli carefully and cook it in abundant salted water. Drain while still firm but reserve the water to be used for cooking the pasta.

Soak the raisins in a small cup with lukewarm water.

Heat some olive oil and add the chopped garlic.

Clean the salt off the anchovies and blend them into the oil. Add the broccoli and let the sauce simmer (adding a little hot, salted water if necessary).

Shortly before removing from the heat, season to taste, and flavour with hot red pepper. Add the pine nuts and raisins, which have been well-drained and squeezed dry.

Cook the orecchiette, drain when al dente, stir into the sauce and flavour with grated or finely cubed pecorino.

Tagliatelle with Asparagus

400 g tagliatelle (recipe on page 122), 2 bunches of asparagus, 2 teaspoons lemon juice, 2.5 dl milk, nutmeg, extra-virgin olive oil, salt and pepper

Clean the asparagus, slice the tips and the soft part of the stalks, and sauté in a few tablespoons of oil. Add salt, pepper, nutmeg and a little less than ½ a glass of hot water.

Cover and simmer over moderate heat for 15 minutes; as soon as the water has dried up, add the lemon juice.

Cook the asparagus until tender, adding milk from time to time. Mix the sauce in a blender, heat again, and stir in with the cooked tagliatelle.

Wild asparagus can also be used for this dish. Gather it only in unpolluted areas, and use only the tenderest parts.

400 g pasta (any
short pasta will do),
250 g ricotta,
4 artichokes,
1 shallot,
1 clove garlic,
1 lemon, 1 small
bunch parsley,
dry white wine,
extra-virgin olive oil,
grated Parmesan
cheese, salt and
pepper

Pasta with Ricotta and Artichokes

Pare the stem and remove the sharp tips from the outer leaves of the artichokes, cut into fine wedges, and soak in water diluted with lemon juice.

Finely chop the shallot and garlic, and sauté in several tablespoons of oil. Drain the artichokes and add to the pan, stirring constantly over high heat.

After a few minutes, lower the heat and add some white wine. Let it evaporate. Season with salt and pepper, cover and simmer about 20 minutes. If necessary, add a little hot, salted water.

Boil the pasta and drain it when al dente. Transfer to the pan with the sauce, add the crumbled ricotta, a few tablespoons of Parmesan and a sprinkling of finely chopped parsley.

Mix well and let the cheese melt a little before turning off the heat. Serve piping hot.

Penne all'Arrabbiata

400 g penne,
500 g ripe and firm tomatoes,
2 cloves garlic, grated pecorino, extra-virgin olive oil, salt,
1 hot red pepper

Blanch the tomatoes in hot water, peel, remove the seeds and chop. Sauté the garlic clove in several tablespoons of oil.

Add the tomatoes and let the sauce thicken over moderate heat, season with salt and the crumbled hot red pepper. Cook for a further 20 minutes over moderate heat.

Cook the pasta in plenty of boiling, salted water and drain when al dente.

Mix into the sauce, turn up the heat for a few seconds, and sprinkle with grated pecorino. Remove from the heat and serve.

Reginette alla Parmigiana

400 g reginette,
150 g fresh grated
Parmesan cheese,
100 g butter,
a few sage leaves,
1 clove garlic,
nutmeg, salt and
pepper

Prepare the sauce while the pasta is cooking in salted water.

Over low heat, melt the butter, add the sage leaves and the crushed garlic clove. As soon as the butter has melted and is beginning to colour (do not let it turn dark brown), remove from the heat and discard the aromatic herbs. Dilute the melted butter with a few tablespoons of cooking water from the pasta, and add the grated Parmesan, mixing well to blend. Flavour with a little salt and grated nutmeg.

Drain the reginette when al dente and transfer to the pan with the Parmesan sauce. Turn up the heat.

Stir well to blend all the ingredients, add a little freshly ground pepper, remove from the heat, and serve.

Spaghetti alla Norma

400 g spaghetti,
600 g tomato
pulp, 100 g grated
mature ricotta,
3 aubergines, 1 onion,
a few basil leaves,
extra-virgin olive oil,
salt, ground hot red
pepper

Clean the aubergines and cut into slices about 1 cm thick; sprinkle with salt, and leave for two hours on paper towels to eliminate the bitter juices. Rinse, dry well, cut into cubes and fry in oil. Leave to dry on paper towels.

Chop the onion and sauté it in several table-spoons of oil. Add the tomatoes, season with salt and hot red pepper, and let thicken over moderate heat.

Boil the pasta, drain when al dente, and transfer to a serving bowl. Mix with the tomato sauce, the fried aubergines, the grated mature ricotta and the crushed basil leaves. Mix thoroughly and serve.

400 g spaghetti,
4 cloves garlic,
1 glass extra-virgin
olive oil, salt,
1 hot red pepper

Spaghetti Aglio, Olio e Peperoncino

Considered something of a 'classic', this recipe, one of the quickest and easiest to prepare, is certain to be a success.

Boil the pasta in plenty of salted water. In the meantime, sauté in a pan the crushed hot red pepper and the finely chopped garlic in a few tablespoons of oil.

For a sauce that is less spicy, remove the hot red pepper from the oil before adding the garlic. For a more delicate garlic taste, let the garlic flavour the oil but remove it before heating the oil with the hot red pepper.

Sedanini and Zucchini

Clean the zucchini and slice it in rounds. Slice the garlic. Heat some oil in a pan, and sauté the sliced garlic and zucchini. Stir carefully to avoid breaking the zucchini. Add salt and pepper, and sprinkle with chopped parsley or mint.

Boil the pasta in plenty of salted water, drain when al dente and transfer to the pan with the zucchini.

Mix the pasta with the sauce, adding a little cream if desired, and serve with abundant grated Parmesan.

400 g sedanini,
500 g zucchini,
1 clove garlic,
a bunch parsley
or mint, cream
(optional),
extra-virgin olive oil,
grated Parmesan
cheese, salt and
pepper

400 g fusilli,
400 g endives,
2 pomegranates,
150 g ricotta,
extra-virgin olive oil,
salt and pepper

Fusilli with Endive and Pomegranate

Clean the endive and cut into strips. Boil in salted water with the pasta.

Meanwhile, in a warmed dish, mix the ricotta with two spoonfuls of hot water from the pasta pot. Season with salt and pepper, and blend the pomegranate seeds into the mixture.

Drain the pasta and endives and transfer to the serving bowl, mixing carefully with the ricotta and pomegranate. Drizzle with the oil.

Tagliolini with Mascarpone

400 g tagliolini
(recipe on page 122),
150 g mascarpone
cheese, 3 egg yolks,
4-5 tablespoons of
grated Parmesan
cheese, grated
nutmeg, salt and
pepper

Prepare the pasta base for the tagliolini, according to the Basic Recipes.

This sauce should be prepared just a few minutes before cooking the pasta. Have the eggs at room temperature. In a saucepan, mix the yolks with the grated Parmesan, a pinch of salt and a grind of fresh pepper, stirring to form a smooth cream.

Place the saucepan over very low heat, or better still, in a double-boiler (or bain-marie). Stirring carefully, add the mascarpone and season with the grated nutmeg.

Boil the pasta, drain it while still al dente, pour it into the sauce, and mix well.

To give this dish a touch of refinement, garnish it at the moment of serving with a little lumpfish roe (or real caviar) and a sprinkle of grated lemon peel.

Vermicelli with Leeks

400 g vermicelli,
4 medium-size leeks,
1 tomato,
2 teaspoons tamari
sauce, extra-virgin
olive oil, salt

Clean the leeks carefully, removing the tougher green parts, and cut into slices of about 1 cm. Sauté the slices briefly in a saucepan in a little oil, then cover and simmer over low heat for about 10 minutes.

Wash and coarsely chop the tomato; add it to the leeks along with a glass of hot water, the tamari sauce and a pinch of salt. Continue to simmer for 20 minutes.

Boil the pasta, draining it while still al dente, then pour over it the piping hot sauce. Mix and serve immediately.

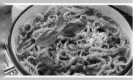

Trenette
with Pesto

400 g trenette,
about 30 basil
leaves, 1 clove garlic,
2-4 teaspoons
pine nuts,
2 teaspoons grated
pecorino cheese,
2 teaspoons grated
Parmesan cheese,
extra-virgin olive
oil, salt

Wash and dry the basil leaves, then grind them in a stone mortar with the garlic and pine nuts (pressing the basil against the sides with circular movements rather than pounding it).

Continue grinding the ingredients, then add the grated cheeses and a pinch of salt.

As soon as you have a smooth paste, add olive oil drop by drop, stirring with the pestle like a spoon to form a thick, creamy sauce. If you prefer, pesto can also be made successfully in a blender.

Boil the trenette in plenty of salted water, drain them when still al dente, and dress with the pesto sauce diluted with one tablespoon of the cooking water. Mix well and serve.

After a GOOD
DINNER,
one can forgive
ANYBODY,
EVEN one's **RELATIVES.**
Oscar Wilde

FRESH
PASTA
AND GNOCCHI

pasta base for
cannelloni
(recipe on page 121)

FOR THE FILLING
500 g spinach,
250 g ricotta
cheese, 2 eggs,
béchamel (recipe on
page 123), grated
Parmesan cheese,
butter, grated
nutmeg, salt and
pepper

Cannelloni Ricotta e Spinaci

Prepare the pasta base for the cannelloni, and continue with the béchamel, according to the Basic Recipes.

Then prepare the spinach and ricotta cheese filling. Wash, trim, and boil the spinach in a little salted water; drain and let cool. Squeeze well, and chop finely.

Mash the ricotta thoroughly in a bowl, and mix it with the spinach, egg yolks, and a few tablespoons of grated Parmesan. Season with salt, pepper and grated nutmeg.

If the mixture is too stiff, add the egg whites or a drop of warm milk, then use the filling to stuff the pasta squares. Roll up the squares, and place them in an oven dish with a layer of béchamel on the bottom.

Pour the rest of the béchamel over, sprinkle with grated Parmesan and dot with butter. Brown in a preheated oven at 356 °F (180 °C) for about half an hour.

pasta base for
cannelloni
(recipe on page 121)

FOR THE FILLING
300 g ground beef,
100 g tomato pulp,
1 onion, basil,
1/2 glass red wine,
2 eggs,
100 g grated
Parmesan cheese,
butter, extra-virgin
olive oil, salt and
pepper

FOR THE SAUCE
béchamel
(recipe on page 123,
half-quantity)

Cannelloni
al Ragù

Prepare the pasta base for the cannelloni, and continue with the béchamel, according to the Basic Recipes.

Then prepare the ground beef and tomato filling. In a saucepan, soften the chopped onion in a little oil, then add the ground beef, stirring so that it browns evenly. Pour in the wine, let it evaporate, season with salt and pepper, and add the tomato pulp.

Cook for about 30 minutes, and add basil before removing from the heat. Let it cool, then blend in the eggs and the Parmesan.

Stuff the cannelloni with this filling, then put them in an oven dish with a thin layer of béchamel on the bottom.

Pour the rest of the sauce over the cannelloni, sprinkle with grated Parmesan and chopped basil, and dot with a bit of butter.

Brown in a preheated oven at 356 °F (180 °C) for about half an hour.

Cannelloni with Salmon

Prepare the pasta base for the cannelloni, and continue with the béchamel, according to the Basic Recipes.

Scald the diced zucchini and the asparagus tips in boiling salted water, then drain them well. In the blender, blend the raw salmon meat, zucchini, asparagus tips, egg and a pinch of salt.

Pour the mixture into a bowl, stir in the ricotta and mix thoroughly.

Cook the pasta, drain, and lay to dry on a tea cloth. Place the squares on a floured surface, spread them with the filling and roll them up.

Arrange the cannelloni in a buttered oven dish, pour the béchamel over them and dot with butter. Brown in a preheated oven 356 °F (180 °C) for about 15 minute before serving.

pasta base for cannelloni
(recipe on page 121)

FOR THE SAUCE
1 cup béchamel
(recipe on page 123),
butter

FOR THE FILLING
400 g salmon meat,
2 zucchini,
12 asparagus stems,
1 egg, 100 g ricotta cheese, salt

Semolina Gnocchi

250 g semolina,
1 l milk, 2 egg yolks,
150 g butter,
100 g grated
Parmesan cheese,
a few sage leaves,
grated nutmeg, salt

Pour the milk and half a litre of water into a large pot with a pinch of salt. Heat, and when it begins to boil, sprinkle in the semolina, beating constantly to avoid lumps.

Cook for about ten minutes, remove from the heat and let cool slightly. Then stir in the egg yolks, a pinch of nutmeg and a little Parmesan, blending thoroughly.

Pour the mixture onto a counter (preferably marble), spread about 1 cm thick using a spatula, then let cool. Using a special cutter, or a glass with moistened rim, cut into circles (or if you prefer, ovals) and arrange slightly overlapping in a buttered ovenproof dish.

Sprinkle generously with grated Parmesan and a few chopped sage leaves, dot with flakes of butter and brown in a hot oven (392 °F, 200 °C) for about 15 minutes.

Potato Agnolotti

FOR THE PASTA
(recipe on page 122)

FOR THE FILLING
600 g potatoes,
1 onion, 3 mint
leaves, 1 pinch
cinnamon, 1 shot
cognac, butter, salt
and pepper

FOR THE SAUCE
grated smoked
ricotta cheese,
butter

Prepare the pasta for the agnolotti following the instructions given in the Basic Recipes (Pasta base for fresh filled pasta).

Boil, peel and mash the potatoes, then stir in the salt and pepper, the cognac, chopped mint and a pinch of cinnamon. Mix the ingredients well. Then slice the onion finely, sauté lightly in a little butter and blend into the potato mixture.

Roll the pasta out in a large sheet. Place piles of the filling at equal distances over half of it, fold over the other half, and press down with your fingertips around each filled section. Cut out the agnolotti with a pastry wheel.

Bring a large pot of water to the boil, salt lightly and drop in the agnolotti. Drain and serve dressed with the melted butter, and sprinkled with the grated smoked ricotta.

Spinach Dumplings

Among the many different recipes for dumplings we have chosen this one, since it is the most suitable for serving without broth.

Start by dicing the stale bread and soaking it in warm milk. Trim and wash the spinach, then boil it in a little salted water or steam it.

Chop the garlic and onion and sauté in a large saucepan in a little butter. Add the drained and squeezed spinach and continue to sauté over moderate heat.

In a large bowl, mix the beaten eggs with the bread, add the spinach and blend thoroughly. Season with salt, a pinch of pepper and the grated nutmeg, then stir in the flour and bread-crumbs.

Shape the mixture into small dumplings, drop them into a large pot of boiling salted water and cook for 15 minutes with the water boiling gently.

Remove with a slotted spoon, serve dressed with the melted butter and sprinkled with grated Parmesan.

300 g stale bread,
800 g spinach,
1 glass milk,
2 eggs, 1 small
onion, 1 clove garlic,
2 teaspoons flour,
1 1/2 tablespoons
breadcrumbs,
2 tablespoons grated
Parmesan cheese,
1 pinch grated
nutmeg,
100 g butter, salt
and pepper

95

pasta base for lasagne
(recipe on page 121)

FOR THE FILLING
2 mozzarellas, grated
Parmesan cheese,
béchamel (recipe on
page 123), butter, salt

FOR THE SAUCE
150 g ground beef,
50 g cooked ham
in a single slice
50 g sausage,
600 g tomato pulp,
1/2 onion, 1 small
carrot, 1/2 celery stalk,
1 clove garlic, bay leaf,
basil, 1 clove,
1 cinnamon stick,
1/2 glass red wine,
extra-virgin olive oil,
salt and pepper

Classic Baked Lasagne

Prepare the pasta, according to the basic recipe, boil it and lay to dry on a tea cloth.

Then prepare the sauce. Clean and chop the onion, carrot, celery, garlic, and the ham. Break up the sausage with a fork and sauté it lightly in a saucepan with a little oil. Add the chopped vegetables and ham, mix well, and let them wilt.

Before the sauce begins to colour, add the ground beef and brown evenly, stirring constantly. Pour in the wine, let it evaporate, then add the tomato, bay leaf, spices and salt.

Lower the heat, cover, and simmer slowly for about 1 hour. The sauce should be fairly liquid, since it is to be poured over the layers of pasta.

While the meat sauce is cooking, prepare the béchamel, according to the basic recipe.

Put a little meat sauce and a little béchamel in the bottom of a rectangular oven dish; blend them with a wooden spoon.

Spread over this a first layer of lasagne, and sprinkle over it diced mozzarella and grated

Parmesan. Cover with another layer of lasagne, then spread with meat sauce and béchamel.

Continue alternating the layers in this manner, until all the ingredients are used up, finishing with a layer of meat sauce and béchamel.

Sprinkle with Parmesan, dot with bits of butter, and bake in a preheated oven (392 °F, 200 °C) for 30-40 minutes.

97

FOR THE PASTA
to the basic recipe
on page 121 add
300 g spinach

FOR THE SAUCE
150 g Castelmagno
cheese,
150 g Dolcelatte
cheese, 150 g fresh
ricotta cheese,
40 g butter, grated
Parmesan cheese,
salt, grated nutmeg,
pepper

Green Lasagne with Cheese Sauce

For the pasta, follow the instructions in the Basic Recipes. Boil the spinach, drain, squeeze and process in the blender, then mix with the pasta dough.

Over very low heat, melt the butter, Dolcelatte and Castelmagno in a saucepan.

Boil the pasta, and spread a first layer in a buttered ovenproof dish.

Cover with a layer of the melted cheese sauce and then with one of ricotta, seasoning with a pinch of nutmeg and a grind of pepper. Continue layering the pasta and cheeses until all the ingredients are used up.

Dot the top layer with a few flakes of butter, and sprinkle generously with grated Parmesan.

Brown in a preheated oven at 392°F (200 °C) for 30-40 minutes, then serve.

Tortellini with Meat Filling

Grind the meat and brown in a saucepan with a tablespoon of butter, then place it in a bowl with the chopped ham and chopped mortadella. Blend together with the 2 eggs, add the grated Parmesan and season with a pinch of grated nutmeg, salt and pepper.

Make the pasta following the basic recipe (Pasta base for fresh filled pasta).

Roll it into a thin sheet, cut it into squares of about 4-5 cm (as you become more expert, you will be able to make even smaller tortellini) and heap a little of the filling on each one.

Fold the opposite corners together to form a triangle, seal the edges well, then roll it around your finger and pinch the two ends together, turning the upper edge outwards.

Cook the tortellini in boiling salted water, or better still in hot meat stock.

Drain and serve with a meat sauce, or if you prefer simply with melted butter flavoured with a few sage leaves.

FOR THE PASTA
recipe on page 122

FOR THE FILLING
100 g chicken breast, 100 g pork loin, 100 g veal, 150 g Parma ham, 1 fairly thick slice Mortadella sausage, 100 g grated Parmesan cheese, 2 eggs, butter, nutmeg, salt and pepper

FOR THE PASTA
300 g pizzoccheri
(recipe on page 120)

FOR THE SAUCE
150 g grated
Parmesan cheese,
150 g soft cheese
(Fontina or Bitto),
200 g white
cabbage or spinach
beet,
200 g potatoes,
3 cloves garlic,
1 sprig sage,
100 g butter,
extra-virgin olive
oil, salt

Baked
Pizzoccheri

Wash the cabbage and potatoes, cut them in pieces and boil both in plenty of salted water.

Put the pizzoccheri to boil in the same water, calculating the cooking times so that all the ingredients can be drained al dente at the same time.

Meanwhile, cut the soft cheese into thin slices and melt the butter with a few spoonfuls of oil, flavouring with the sage and the crushed garlic cloves (removing the latter as soon as they begin to colour).

Spread a first layer of pasta and vegetables in an ovenproof dish. Sprinkle with grated Parmesan and the slices of soft cheese, and season with the sage flavoured butter.

Continue building up these layers, then complete with a generous sprinkling of Parmesan and dot with a few flakes of butter.

Crisp in a preheated oven at 392°F (200 °C) for about 10 minutes.

Bergamo-Style Casoncelli

FOR THE PASTA
500 g white flour,
1 pinch salt, 5 eggs

FOR THE FILLING
300 g beef, 1 carrot,
1 small celery stalk,
1/2 onion, 1 clove,
1 pinch grated
nutmeg, 3-4 basil
leaves, 1 egg yolk,
1/2 glass full-bodied
red wine,
50 g grated
Parmesan cheese,
50 g fine
breadcrumbs, butter,
1 1/2 tablespoons
extra-virgin olive oil,
salt and pepper

FOR THE SAUCE
a few sage leaves,
100 g grated Grana
cheese, 120 g butter

On a floured board, mix the flour with a pinch of salt, four whole eggs and one yolk, adding a little water if necessary. Knead well for about ten minutes, then roll two thin sheets, being careful not to let them dry out.

In a saucepan, sauté the thinly sliced onion in a rounded tablespoon of butter and the olive oil. Add the beef and brown it on all sides, then sprinkle with the wine and let it evaporate.

Clean and chop the carrot and celery. Add them to the saucepan with the meat, along with the clove, chopped basil, salt, pepper and a pinch of grated nutmeg.

Simmer covered for two and a half hours, adding a little hot water from time to time if necessary.

When done, dice the meat and pass the vegetables through a food mill. Pour the meat and vegetables into a bowl, add the breadcrumbs, the grated Grana and the egg yolk. Blend all the ingredients thoroughly, and salt to taste.

Place small heaps of this mixture at equal distances on one sheet of pasta.

Lay the second sheet over the first and press down with your fingertips around each filled section to seal thoroughly. Use a pastry wheel to cut it into squares about 4 cm. Let them dry on a lightly floured tea cloth.

Cook the casoncelli in plenty of boiling salted water for about 10 minutes, drain thoroughly, and pour into a hot serving dish, dress with the melted butter flavoured with sage, and sprinkle with grated Grana.

Let the flavours blend for a few seconds before serving.

Potato Gnocchi with Tomatoes

FOR THE GNOCCHI
1 kg potatoes,
200 g white flour,
salt

FOR THE SAUCE
500 g tomato pulp,
1 onion, butter,
salt and pepper

Boil the potatoes in their skins, then peel and wait for them to be completely cold, then mash them. Place the mashed potatoes on a floured surface; lightly incorporate the salt and enough flour to produce the right consistency. (Soft, fluffy gnocchi are made by using only a little flour). Roll the mixture into finger-size sausages, cut into pieces, and give them the typical gnocchi shape by lightly pushing them against the back of a fork.

Prepare the sauce: put the tomato pulp and the onion, cut into wedges, into a large saucepan with a tablespoon of butter, salt and pepper. Cook over moderate heat for about 15 minutes, then switch off and remove the onions.

Bring a large pot of salted water to the boil and drop in the gnocchi a few at a time. As soon as they rise to the surface, remove with a slotted spoon and serve directly on the dinner plates, spooning the tomato sauce over. Serve the grated Parmesan separately.

Gnocchi can be served with various sauces: tomato, meat sauce, pesto, a sauce made with four different kinds of cheese or cream and walnuts.

Crepes with Red Chicory Filling

FOR 12 CREPES
2.5 dl milk,
125 g flour, 2 eggs,
30 g butter, salt

FOR THE FILLING
600 g red chicory,
1 onion, béchamel
(recipe on page 123),
grated Parmesan
cheese, dry white
wine, salt and pepper

To prepare the crepes, melt the butter over low heat. Beat the eggs, flour and a pinch of salt with an egg-whisk, then, continuing to whisk, dilute with the milk and the melted butter.

Wash and slice the onion and chicory, then sauté lightly in a saucepan with a little oil. Sprinkle the vegetables with white wine, season with salt and pepper, lower the heat and simmer for another 10 minutes.

Prepare the béchamel and mix half of it with the chicory and onion.

Fill the crepes with this mixture, then fold them in four and arrange slightly overlapping in a buttered ovenproof dish. Pour the rest of the béchamel over them, sprinkle with grated Parmesan, and dot with bits of butter.

Brown in a hot oven at 356 °F (180 °C).

Spinach
Gnocchi

1 kg spinach,
350 g ricotta
cheese, 2 egg yolks,
grated Parmesan
cheese, flour, a few
sage leaves, butter,
grated nutmeg, salt
and pepper

Clean the spinach well; boil it in a little salted water, drain and squeeze thoroughly, then chop finely.

In a bowl, mash the ricotta with a fork, add the spinach, and bind together with the egg yolks and 1 ½ tablespoons of Parmesan, seasoning with salt, pepper and grated nutmeg.

With the help of a teaspoon, shape the mixture into balls about the size of a walnut and roll them in flour, then drop them into a large pot of boiling salted water.

As soon as they come to the surface, remove them carefully with a slotted spoon.

Serve with melted butter flavoured with sage and sprinkled with grated Parmesan.

FOR THE PASTA
(recipe on page 122)

FOR THE FILLING
250 g asparagus
tips, 100 g fresh
ricotta cheese,
100 g grated
Parmesan cheese,
1 egg, salt and
pepper

FOR THE SAUCE
40 g butter, 1 sprig
rosemary, grated
Parmesan cheese

Asparagus Ravioloni

For the pasta, follow the instructions given in the Basic Recipes (Pasta base for fresh filled pasta).

Steam the asparagus tips and set about 20 of them aside for the sauce. Chop the rest and mix them in a bowl with the ricotta, the grated Parmesan and the egg, then season with salt and pepper.

Blend the mixture well, then place teaspoonfuls of it at equal distances over half the sheet of rolled out pasta. Fold over the pasta, pressing down with your fingertips around the filled sections, then cut into squares of about 4 cm.

In a small saucepan, melt and lightly colour the butter, flavouring it with the rosemary.

In another saucepan, lightly sauté the remaining 20 asparagus tips.

Cook the ravioloni in plenty of boiling salted water, drain and pour into a serving dish.

Dress with the melted butter, sprinkle with the asparagus tips and grated Parmesan, and serve.

Gnocchi Gratin

1 kg potatoes,
3 eggs,
1 cup béchamel
(recipe on page 123),
2 1/2 tablespoons of
table cream, grated
Parmesan cheese,
80 g butter, salt

Choose suitable floury potatoes. Boil them, then peel and mash them while still hot. Stir in the salt, 2 eggs, 50 g butter and 2 tablespoons of grated Parmesan, blending thoroughly.

Spread the mixture on a buttered surface, levelling it out about 1 cm thick, and let it cool. Then cut out disks, using a special cutter or a glass with moistened rim.

Prepare the béchamel according to the basic recipe.

Butter an ovenproof dish and arrange the gnocchi in layers, covering each layer with béchamel and grated Parmesan. Brown in a hot oven (392 °F, 200 °C) for about 10 minutes.

Tortelloni Ricotta e Spinaci

Prepare the pasta following the instructions given in the Basic Recipes (Pasta base for fresh filled pasta).

Pass the ricotta through a sieve. Boil the spinach in a little salted water, drain, squeeze thoroughly and chop.

Place the ricotta and spinach in a bowl; blend in the eggs, chopped parsley and grated Parmesan, seasoning the mixture with salt, pepper and a pinch of grated nutmeg. Mix all of the ingredients to form a smooth cream.

Roll the pasta into a thin sheet and cut out disks of about 8 cm. Place a small heap of filling at the centre of each disk, then fold in half to form half-moon shapes, sealing the edges well.

Cook in plenty of boiling salted water. When done, drain, and dress with the melted butter flavoured with a few sage leaves.

Sprinkle generously with grated Parmesan and serve immediately.

FOR THE PASTA
(recipe on page 122)

FOR THE FILLING
300 g spinach, 300 g ricotta cheese, 1 bunch parsley, 2 eggs, grated nutmeg, 50 g grated Parmesan cheese, salt and pepper

FOR THE SAUCE
a few sage leaves, 100 g grated Parmesan cheese, butter

111

Zucchini Ravioloni

FOR THE PASTA
(Pasta base for fresh filled pasta, recipe on page 122)

FOR THE FILLING
200 g zucchini, 150 g ricotta cheese, grated Parmesan cheese, butter, grated nutmeg, salt and pepper

FOR THE SAUCE
4 ripe and firm tomatoes, a few basil leaves, 1 leek, a few sage leaves, 40 g butter, extra-virgin olive oil, grated Parmesan cheese, salt and pepper

Prepare the pasta following the basic recipe.

Clean the zucchini, slice them thinly and sauté lightly in a little butter, seasoning with salt and grated nutmeg. Pass them through a sieve. Place the pureed zucchini in a bowl with the ricotta and a handful of grated Parmesan.

Make the ravioloni by arranging heaps of the mixture about the size of a walnut over half the sheet of rolled out pasta. Fold over the other half and press down with your fingertips around the filled sections, then use a pastry wheel to cut out squares of about 4 cm.

Chop the leek finely and sauté it in a little oil. Blanch the tomatoes in boiling water for a few minutes, peel, seed and chop them, and add them to the leek with a pinch of salt. Leave to reduce, and in another small saucepan melt the butter, flavouring it with a few sage leaves.

Cook the ravioloni in plenty of boiling salted water, drain well and transfer to a serving dish. Pour the tomato sauce and the melted butter over them and mix. Garnish with chopped basil, sprinkle with grated Parmesan, and serve.

112

FOR THE TORTELLI
40 g white flour,
1 kg bumpy yellow
pumpkin,
100 g macaroons,
150 g grated
Parmesan cheese,
5 eggs, grated
nutmeg, salt

FOR THE SAUCE
butter, a few sage
leaves, Parmesan
cheese

Pumpkin Tortelli with Sage Butter

Remove the rind and seeds from the pumpkin and cook it in the oven. Sieve the pulp into a bowl and blend in one egg, the crumbled macaroons and the grated Parmesan, seasoning with salt and nutmeg.

Mix the flour with the remaining eggs and a pinch of salt, kneading well until you have a firm, even dough. Roll out into a thin sheet, then cut it into squares.

Place a little of the pumpkin filling at the centre of each, then fold over the pasta, sealing the edges well.

In al small pot, melt the butter, flavouring it with a few sage leaves.

Cook the tortelli in plenty of boiling salted water, drain, and serve dressed with the flavoured butter and sprinkled with grated Parmesan.

In Lombardy, this filling is made with the addition of about 100 g of Cremona mustard (candied fruit in a mustard syrup), with the fruit chopped in the syrup.

Potato Tortelloni

Boil the potatoes, peel and mash them, then mix them with the flour. Blend in the eggs, a pinch of salt and a little of the potato cooking water, and knead into a pliable dough.

Roll flat on a floured surface and cut into strips of about 10 cm. In the lower half of each strip, place small heaps of the finely diced cheeses at equal distances. Fold over the top half of the strip, pressing the edges down well. Cut out the tortelloni using the special cutter, or a glass with lightly moistened rim.

Bring a large pot of salted water to the boil, drop in the tortelloni and cook briefly until they come to the surface.

Drain and transfer to a warm serving dish, dress with the melted butter, sprinkle with grated Parmesan, and serve.

FOR THE PASTA
500 g wheat flour, 200 g floury potatoes, 3 eggs, salt

FOR THE FILLING
400 g mixed cheese (ricotta, Gorgonzola, Emmental etc)

FOR THE SAUCE
grated Parmesan cheese, butter

Strangolapreti

FOR THE PASTA
300 g spinach,
2 stale bread rolls,
3 1/2 tablespoons
white flour,
2 eggs, milk, salt

FOR THE SAUCE
butter, a few sage
leaves, grated
Parmesan cheese

Strangolapreti is a typical Alto Adige dish, which can also be made with nettles, spinach beet or wild spinach.

Clean the spinach carefully, wash it, and steam or cook in a small amount of boiling water, then drain, squeeze and chop finely.

In the meantime, crumble the bread into a bowl, moistening it with a little milk. Add the eggs, the flour and a pinch of salt and mix well. Lastly, add the spinach and shape the mixture into gnocchi about the size of a large walnut.

Bring a large pot of salted water to the boil and cook the gnocchi until they come to the surface. It's best to cook the gnocchi a few at a time, to keep them from sticking together.

Drain carefully, then dress with the melted butter, flavoured with a few sage leaves and the grated cheese.

ORECCHIETTE

160 g extra-fine flour, 240 g durum wheat flour, water, salt.

Orecchiette is a pasta typical of Puglia (a southern region of Italy).
Mix the two flours on a breadboard and make a mound with a well in the centre. Add a pinch of salt and enough water to mix and knead into a smooth, elastic dough. Knead thoroughly for about 10 minutes until the water is absorbed, then roll the dough out into long sausages and cut into pieces about 1 cm long.
Using a round-bladed knife, flatten each cylinder into a shell-shape on a floured breadboard, then form into 'little ears' by moulding them over the tip of your thumb. Leave them to dry on lightly floured tea cloths.

PICI

400 g extra-fine flour, extra-virgin olive oil, water, salt.

This typical Sienese pasta is a kind of homemade spaghetti. Pici are made by hand and rolled out on a breadboard, and the most expert housewives can roll them up to two metres long!
Heap the flour at the centre of the breadboard, add 2 teaspoons of extra-virgin olive oil, a pinch of salt, and enough water to mix the dough. Knead energetically, adding a little warm water gradually if required.
When you have a firm, smooth dough, roll it into a ball, brush the surface with oil, and let it rest, covered with a tea cloth, for about half an hour. Then roll it into a sheet about 1.5 cm thick and cut into thin 3 mm strips, rolling them with well-floured hands into the shape of spaghetti. As you prepare the pici, place them to dry on a tea cloth dusted with flour or semolina to keep them from sticking together.

PIZZOCCHERI

250 g buckwheat flour, 150 g extra-fine flour, water, salt and pepper.

Mix the two kinds of flours on a floured breadboard and make a mound with a well in the centre. Add a pinch of salt and enough water to blend. Knead thoroughly until you have a firm, elastic dough. With a rolling-pin, roll out a sheet about 1.5 mm thick, and cut into strips about 1 cm wide and 7 cm long.

BIGOLI

250 g extra-fine flour, 150 g durum wheat flour, 4 eggs, water, salt.

Pile the two kinds of flour in the middle of the breadboard, make a well in the centre, break the eggs into it and add a pinch of salt. Work the eggs into the flour, adding a little water if the mixture is too dry. Knead thoroughly to form a smooth, elastic dough. Put the dough through the pasta mill, using a wheel with 3 mm holes, then cut the bigoli into lengths of 20 cm with a knife.

Leave the pasta to dry on a floured tea cloth for several hours before using.

GARGANELLI

250 g extra-fine flour, 150 g durum wheat flour, 2 whole eggs and 1 yolk, salt.

Mix the two types of flour on the breadboard. Make a well in the centre and break in 2 whole eggs and 1 yolk along with a pinch of salt. Mix thoroughly and knead until you have a smooth, elastic dough. Use a rolling-pin and roll out a sheet about 1 mm thick, then cut it into 6 cm squares. Roll these up diagonally around a wooden stick about the size of a pencil, pressing them with your fingertips. Then mark the garganelli using the special tool known as a comb, remove them, and lay them out to dry.

TROFIE

400 g extra-fine flour, water, salt.

Pour the flour onto the breadboard, add a pinch of salt and enough water to mix. Knead thoroughly with your hands until you have a dense, smooth, elastic dough. Break off pieces about the size of a bean, roll them into thin sausages, then, with well-floured hands, twist them into corkscrew shapes. Leave them to dry on a flour-sprinkled tea cloth for four hours before cooking.

PASTA BASE FOR CANNELLONI

500 g extra-fine flour, 4 eggs, 2 teaspoons extra-virgin olive oil, salt.

Mound the flour onto the breadboard, make a well in the centre and break in the eggs, adding a pinch of salt and 2 teaspoons of extra-virgin olive oil. Rub in well, then knead to form a smooth, elastic dough. Leave covered in a damp tea cloth for about half an hour, then knead again. With a rolling-pin, roll out sheets about 1 mm thick. Use a knife to cut the pasta into squares of about 12 cm. Cook the squares of pasta a few at a time, draining them while still al dente. Lay them out singly on a damp tea cloth to dry.

PASTA BASE FOR LASAGNE

500 g extra-fine flour, 4 eggs, 2 teaspoons extra-virgin olive oil, salt.

Add the eggs to the flour along with a pinch of salt and 2 teaspoons of extra-virgin olive oil. Mix well, then knead thoroughly with your hands to form a smooth, elastic dough. Leave the dough covered with a damp tea cloth for about half an hour, then knead it again and roll out a sheet about 1.5 mm thick. Leave to rest for about 15 minutes, then use a knife to cut out squares of about 10 cm (the size varies according to requirements). Let the squares of pasta dry for at least a couple of hours before cooking. Cook the lasagne a few at a time, draining them while al dente, and laying them out singly on a damp tea cloth to dry.

PASTA BASE FOR FRESH FILLED PASTA

400 g extra-fine flour, 4 eggs, 2 teaspoons extra-virgin olive oil, salt.

Pour the flour onto the breadboard, make a well in the centre, break in the eggs, adding a pinch of salt and the oil. Mix thoroughly, kneading until you have a smooth, elastic dough. Leave covered with a damp tea cloth for about half an hour, then knead again and roll out in thin sheets with the rolling-pin. This pasta is much easier to work with if it is not allowed to dry out.

TAGLIATELLE, TAGLIOLINI, FETTUCCINE, PAPPARDELLE

500 g extra-fine flour, 4 eggs, 2 teaspoons extra-virgin olive oil, 1 handful cornmeal.

Pour the flour in a heap onto a breadboard. Make a well in the centre, add the eggs with a pinch of salt and the oil. Blend in well and knead thoroughly with your hands until you have a smooth, elastic dough. Leave covered with a damp tea cloth for half an hour, then knead again and roll into thin sheets with the rolling-pin. Sprinkle the dough with the cornmeal and let it rest for a few minutes, then roll it out and cut into strips of the desired width. Tagliatelle are 2 cm wide, fettuccine 1 cm, tagliolini a few millimetres, and pappardelle 3 or 4 cm.

BÉCHAMEL

50 g butter, 50 g flour, 1/2 l milk, 1 pinch grated nutmeg, salt and pepper.

The correct preparation of a béchamel sauce is one of the first hurdles to be faced by any cook. The fear of ending up with a lumpy, tasteless liquid will be gradually overcome with experience, and by learning from mistakes. All it takes is practice, and after a number of attempts you will soon find that you too can make a smooth, tasty béchamel, without even needing to measure the ingredients. In a saucepan, melt the butter gently over low heat. Sprinkle the flour over it and beat it in using an egg-whisk. Heat the milk without letting it boil and use it to dilute the sauce. The milk should be added gradually, stirring constantly, to avoid the formation of the dreaded lumps. Continue stirring rhythmically until you can feel the sauce thickening. As soon as the first boiling bubbles begin to form, count 10 minutes cooking-time, stirring constantly. Just before you switch off the heat, add salt, a grinding of fresh pepper and a pinch of grated nutmeg.

For a thicker sauce, you can increase the quantities of butter and flour (always the same amount of each) while using the same amount of milk, or you can thicken the sauce further by boiling it longer over the heat.

For a very light sauce, milk can be substituted with vegetable stock, or with fish stock for use with fish-based dishes.

RECIPE INDEX

124

RECIPE INDEX

ICONOGRAPHIC REFERENCES

Photographs: Giunti Archives/Giuliano Valsecchi - Florence; Giunti Archives with the exception of:

Giunti Archives: Nicola Grifoni, 16, 38, 58, 86; Roberto Germogli - Firenze, 19, 65; Giovanni Petronio - Firenze, 49; Lorenzo Borri - Firenze, 53; Stockbyte (CD-RF) 85, 89.

Fotolia: ©Sam (pasta pattern image) ©massimhokuto, 9, 17, 39, 59, 87; ©Giuseppe Porzani, 9, 17, 39, 59, 87, 101; ©JCVStock, 9, 16, 38, 58, 86; ©pershing, 9, 16, 38, 58, 86; ©Pixelshop, 10, 12, 14, 16, 38, 58, 86; ©anghifoto, 10, 12, 14, 16, 38, 58, 86; ©Rick Henzel, 11, 13, 15, 17, 39, 59, 87; ©scaliger, 11, 13, 15, 17, 39, 59, 87; ©lapas77, 16, 38, 58, 86; ©Urso Antonio, 16, 38, 58, 86; ©Jenifoto 17, 39, 59, 87; ©ArTo 17, 39, 59, 87; ©goodluz, 59; ©Francesco83, 61; ©Lorenzo Buttitta 69; ©Marco Meyer 73, 97, 105; ©JJAVA 109; ©Comugnero Silvana 103, ©Stefano Neri 118.

Corbis: ©HIROSHI USUI/amanaimages, 39.

Cubo Images: ©Mauritius Images, 17.

Shutterstock: ©Michelangelo Gratton, 87.